THE
DUNES

by

Erin Sands

Lauren,
May this journey
open doors and
be the beginning of a
fresh "Awesome" in your
life. Much love
Erin Sands

ISBN: 0615982948
ISBN 13: 9780615982946

Dedicated to my mother,
Brenda Maria Anderson,
who taught me how to fly

CONTENTS

INTRODUCTION

In life, sometimes the kernels of wisdom and the richness of revelation can be found in the most innocent of stories; and so it is with *The Dunes*.

Join one man and one woman in an exquisitely simple yet remarkably profound journey as you discover with them that the mountain you must climb in order to live the abundant life of your dreams is located squarely within your heart.

Illuminated in seven revelations, *The Dunes* will carry you on a journey to not only examine the obstacles holding you back, but to conquer and overcome them as well. Prepare to enter into your extraordinary self; ready to walk in the promise and purpose that awaits you.

On this journey you will need a *journal* to serve as your growth companion, a place you can record your innermost feelings, fears and beliefs. Your journal can be a simple notebook or a sophisticated diary. The choice is yours. It is key to your success that you take the time to chronicle and reflect on your journey as guided by each of the seven revelations in *The Dunes*.

You can experience *The Dunes* in the recommended seven weeks, exploring one revelation per week, or at a pace that suits you. The goal is to plunge in wholeheartedly and emerge transformed. Ready to experience life anew!

...I am come that they might have life, and that they might have it more abundantly. -John 10:10

Welcome to *The Dunes*!

THE FIRST REVELATION

FEAR

Fear is a bold thief, robbing you of the freedom that exists beyond it, right before your very eyes.

*I*n the heart of the universe, in a land not so far away, exists a place of imminent transformation. It is a place undiscovered by most, and sought out by a daring few, a place where the best and the worst are revealed without filter, and the quest, though formidable, begets a masterpiece of the soul. In this place, a war is waged against the stagnant heart that seeks to cling to what was and cripple new life with old fears. And so it has been that only the brave in spirit venture upon it, content to reap its end result as their reward. Thus believing in *change,* they call this place "The Dunes".

Not for the delicate, The Dunes is a glorious 300-foot-high, 75-degree incline of soft sand that has been bleached by the blazing sun. At first glance, it is awe-inspiring. Its beauty is evident, yet uncompromising, in its call. It is a majestic uphill sand climb resolutely postured as the menacing hurdle to divine destiny. Yet, still they come to answer its call. Still they arrive consumed by the desire to be more than they were when they began, hoping that what lies inside of them is the fullness of life available beyond The Dunes.

Our story begins on a very beautiful and very hot day at The Dunes. It is 105 degrees outside and we find a man and a woman baking in the afternoon sun. One stands at the top of the 300-foot mound, the other, at the bottom.

The One: *I love you.*

The Other: *And I love you.*

The One: *I want you with me. Take this journey, meet me at the top and trust that everything will be all right.*

The Other slowly considered the request and believing that their love was heaven sent elected to rise to the challenge. But wait…

The Other: *Are you certain you want me by your side? The dust from the wind has made me dirty from head to toe, and to be honest, I look awful.*

The One: *The dust is part of the journey; besides, I find you exceptional inside and out. My love sees you clearly and values all that you are.*

Upon hearing this *The Other* eyed the heaping sand dune and decidedly set about the journey, the sanctuary of love now the only goal. But a quarter of the way up—as each step was met with blisters formed by the intense heat of the scorching sand—*The Other* cried out in frustration.

The Other: *This hurts! I am barefoot and the sand is burning my feet. Come down the dune and meet me halfway. Together the journey will be easier.*

The One: *I'm sorry that it's difficult and I hate that you're in pain. But I've lived my whole life from up here. The top of this dune is all I know.*

The Other: *I understand that you're afraid…but if we try, maybe together, we can overcome the unknown.*

The One stood at the top of the dune dumbfounded, sobered by the sudden realization that declarations of love must one day come face to face with the sacrifice needed to justify them. Still, all that was said was…

The One: *I can't.*

Hearing those words, *The Other* stopped. Almost halfway up the hill, feet blistered, eyes stinging from the dirt and tears, *The Other* stopped. Baffled and disgusted in the scorching sun, the experience gave life to a paradox: *The Other* was too in love to turn back and too hurt to take another step forward so instead sought the only refuge that could be found: prayer.

The Other: *Lord, I'm tired. You brought us to The Dunes for a reason. But here we are issue-laden, polar opposites and failing miserably at the promise at hand. What should we do? How do we get past this impasse and to each other?*

GOD: **Stagger not at my promises through fear and unbelief. Instead be strong in faith and in your actions give me glory. When facing all things, be fully persuaded that what I have promised, I am able also to perform—or you can quit.**

The Other: *Um…wait a minute. Did you just say I can quit?*

GOD: **My love gives you a choice. Have faith or quit—the decision is yours to make.**

The Other: *So let me get this straight. I can choose to quit, which forsakes the promise or I can choose faith and walk towards the unknown?*

GOD: **Yes.**

And so for hours, *The Other* sat head in hand, sad and withdrawn, filled with fear at the very notion of continuing to believe in things that had not been seen.

The One: *How long are you going to sit there sulking? When I told you I loved you I meant it. Make it up the hill and our love will see us through the rest.*

And there stood *The One*, the sight reminding *The Other* of the reason the journey even began. And although *The One* was still too afraid to venture down the hill, *The Other* noticed something was different. This time *The One* stood with a rope extended in *The Other's* direction. A mustard seed. *The Other*…got up.

FIRST REVELATION

Commentary

rowing up as an only child I had a vivid imagination coupled with a fierce artistic creativity that my mother fostered with lessons in dance, theatre and gymnastics. I was equally comfortable surrounded by my bevy of friends or in the solitude of my own company where my bedroom became a stage and I performed hits from the movie soundtracks of *Fame*, *Mary Poppins* and *Grease*. I created a world of magic filled with fantasies of stardom.

Every night, equipped with my mirror as the audience and my hairbrush as my mic, I danced and sang to a sold-out crowd of one. I believed that God and I had a special relationship, a secret we alone shared, that one day I would achieve profound greatness through His purpose. I know, pretty ambitious but I was ten years old and, I promise you, I believed it with my whole heart. Then I grew up. Years passed and life didn't quite pan out the way I thought God and I had planned it. In fact, life had pretty much gone rogue on me and God's plan.

I spent my twenties broke and chasing a dream. Much of my thirties, I spent learning some very painful lessons, while still broke and chasing the same dream. By my late thirties, my disappointments mounted by the dozens, my failures seemed to far outweigh my successes and I found myself very depressed. Whenever people shared how talented they thought I was, it secretly broke my heart because it served as a reminder of the promise that hadn't manifested, leaving me with that same haunting question…If I was so great why was I still single in my late thirties, struggling financially, and why, after so many years of dedication and dogged persistence, had my career goals gone unrealized?

Webster's Dictionary defines *promise* as a noun, meaning *to do something specified; an expectation of success.*

So, at the age of thirty-nine, I reached a proverbial fork in the road. I was broke, anxious and uncertain about life. I was sad about not being where I had hoped I'd be and in despair over the thought that my life may never change. I had tried every plan that I knew to try. I had given everything I had to give and all I was surrounded by was the nothing of my results. As cliché as this sounds, with my one last card to play, I dropped to my knees and cried out to God in prayer. This is the scripture He placed on my spirit. Allow me now to share it with you:

Faith is the substance of things hoped for,
*the evidence of things not seen. -*Hebrews 11:1

What?
Wait a minute…Are you kidding me?!!
I had hoped!
I was the queen of hope.
I had believed!
I was freakin' Jiminy Cricket!
I did all of those things and it still hadn't happened yet!
Oh…
…wait a minute…
…"yet".
It hadn't happened,
"yet".
…and then I understood…

Being blessed to love a child, truly love a child, is probably as close as we can come in our humanity to understanding the love of God. When you love a child, you see the best in them, you see their highest potential. We can never be God, but for a moment I want you to picture having a divine, perfect love for a child. It is unconditional, sacrificing and uncompromising in affording him everything he needs to be his best.

Place your child in a garden with nothing but opportunities surrounding him. Now see your child afraid. Instead of enjoying the entire garden and all it has to offer he stands in just a small corner of it, trembling in fear, afraid of every grass hopper and ant that comes his way. You look at him incredulously because you have given him authority over these tiny creatures, and if he were to recognize the strength and breadth of his power, he would laugh and see them for what they truly are: nothing. Nothing in comparison to all you have created him to be. So you gently tell him you love him. You beckon him to step out of the corner of the garden. He looks at you still trembling in fear, afraid to trust you, afraid to step out and possess the land you have given him.

I imagine this is what I looked like to an all-loving, all-powerful God, who, like a sovereign faithful parent, wanted me to step out of that corner and boldly enjoy the fullness of the garden, taking in all of the blessings and the beauty that surrounded me, free from the fear and defeat of my past. And trust it is an insult for us to do anything less.

When I received this revelation in my spirit, I chose to believe again. I became filled with gratitude for what I did have and emboldened with hope for what was to come. That day I made the decision to take God at His word. I released my fears and immersed myself in the garden of life, and after years of "No", my "Yes" finally came.

FIRST REVELATION

Journal Questions

As you answer the journal questions in each revelation, you can use a separate journal as I recommended in the Introduction or you can write your answers directly into the book. It is essential that you are completely open and honest as you answer each of the questions. Journaling is your personal time to reflect, grow and gain insight that will empower you into positive life changes.

1) What is your biggest fear?

2) **In what ways have you allowed this fear to affect your peace and prevent you from accessing all that God has for you?**

_____

_____

_____

_____

_____

_____

_____

_____

_____

_____

_____

_____

_____

_____

_____

_____

_____

_____

_____

_____

_____

_____

_____

_____

In examining the fear you listed in questions one and two, know that at the center of it is either the fear of failure or the fear of what you cannot control. Let's try something! The purpose of the next two questions is to remove the fear of the outcome. Sometimes writing out the full manifestation of our fears allows us to see how nonsensical they are. We are able to gain strength when we can remove the dread from an undesired outcome. Go ahead…give it a try!

3) **Write out the manifestation of this fear in terms of your imagined worst-case scenario. Describe how this failure would look and feel.**

_____

_____

_____

_____

_____

_____

_____

_____

_____

_____

_____

_____

_____

_____

_____

_____

_____

_____

4) Now write out the manifestation of your fear in terms of success. Describe what it would look like and what it would feel like if the best possible result happened.

_____

_____

_____

_____

_____

_____

_____

_____

_____

_____

_____

_____

_____

_____

_____

_____

_____

_____

_____

_____

_____

_____

_____

_____

5) Write about a time in the past when you stepped out boldly on faith. List all of the blessings, challenges and lessons that came as a result. Include what you learned about yourself and God through that experience.

_____

_____

_____

_____

_____

_____

_____

_____

_____

_____

_____

_____

_____

_____

_____

_____

_____

_____

_____

_____

_____

_____

_____

FIRST REVELATION

Challenge

This week do something you have been afraid to do. It can be a small step or a significant leap. Whether it is a meaningful beginning or a profound rebellion against your fear, boldly take a step out of the corner of the garden and begin to possess the land.

FIRST REVELATION

Growth Check

At this point you should have completed **The First Revelation Questions** as well as your **First Revelation Challenge**. Take some time to write in your journal about your experience. Or take a moment to quietly reflect on the following questions:

How did it feel to give voice to your fears and see them written out on paper?

Did it remove some of the anxiety and doubt?

How did it feel to do something that you had previously been afraid to do?

How has it impacted your self-confidence?

I hope you enjoyed The First Revelation Challenge of tackling one of your fears.

As you take this journey it is important to be cognizant of your growth, and your feelings. If you are taking this journey alone, always take the time to pray and write about your progress. If you are taking this journey within the boundaries of a group of people who are also reading The Dunes, *it is important to pray as a group as well as to share your feelings and progress with each other.*

You are doing great! Let's move on to The Second Revelation and peel off another layer.

THE SECOND REVELATION

DECIDE

The first step of every journey,
every lesson
and every victory
begins with a decision.

*U*sing the rope as leverage, *The Other* again set about the journey, feet slightly numb yet more tolerant of the arduous conditions. With every step, *The Other* became more covered in dust. With every moment, *The Other* again began to question if someone so dirty was even worthy of finding love at the top of The Dunes.

The Other: *Lord, you say that I am fearfully and wonderfully made but all I see is a mess. How can I be what's needed of me, when all I feel is shame for all that I'm not…?*

Longing for a reassuring gaze from *The One*, *The Other* looked up and searched the top of the dune but instead saw that the rope had been tied to a fence.

The Other: *Where are you? I can't see you. I need to feel connected to you to maintain the will to reach the goal. Without the connection, my strength wanes and fear sets in. If I can't see you, how am I supposed to feel confident that you still want the promise?*

The One: *Why do you need constant reassuring? I love you. I want you here but I am able to prepare for the promise without the connection.*

Upon hearing this *The Other* fell down in the sand and had a good old-fashioned, grown-up temper tantrum.

The Other: *Why won't you extend yourself to make things comfortable for me at least one time! Why do you only consider your perspective regardless of the pain I'm in? I'm the one traveling up the hill in intense heat and horrendous conditions and yet you can't do this one thing!*

The words of *The Other* served as an awakening for *The One*, and now aware *The One* was driven to decide. It was in this process that *The One* saw *himself* for the first time. The pain and frustration of *The Other* truly affected him and he began to question very seriously if he was capable of making *The Other* happy. Could he really love as Christ loves and give *The Other* the connection that was desired and obviously needed?

You see, in his heart *The One* faced a sand dune all his own and for years he had let it fester unattended. A servant of fear, he had managed to navigate through life dodging that ever-present call to commit to someone in a way that would leave him wide open and vulnerable. Content to accept the lie that "it just hadn't happened yet", he became a mystery even to himself, as he diligently built bridges he would never cross. He became like a child holding a present he was terrified to open.

But now, alone, harnessed with the reality of himself, he began to pray. He prayed for strength, wisdom and clarity. But unlike *The Other* he was vastly familiar with his options, and being a fan of free will he opted for the path of least resistance: apathy. He chose to let *The Other* slip through his fingers. He envisioned the future without the promise of their union and the challenges that came with it.

However, as he began to see his future, despite his efforts, he could not envision it without *The Other*. He tried harder. He saw himself successful with a beautiful home and his dream, state-of-the-art flat screen television. He was surrounded by friends and family but there by his side was *The Other*, laughing, challenging and encouraging him every step of the way. He snapped out of it and tried again. This time he saw himself even more successful. His goals and dreams realized: corporate tycoon, philanthropist and champion of industry. Then in walked *The Other*, great with child and glowing—carrying his legacy, their twin boys! He snapped out of it and laughed to himself. That which he tried so hard to prevent happened anyway—*The Other* was a part of him. With this awareness he called out to her as he untied the rope from the fence.

The One: *Woman, I know who you are. Look into my eyes and get what you need. I am here for you. Make it up the hill and find rest in my devotion.*

The Other, tired of crying and still very much in love, decided not to question but to instead believe. *She* got up.

SECOND REVELATION

Commentary

By the age of twenty-seven I had been dancing and choreographing professionally for over fifteen years. I had been cast in feature films and television shows that made me recognizable in public, so it may surprise you to learn that when I joined the theatrical ministry at my church, my goal was to cater to the background. I wanted to show up unnoticed, watch and not really participate. I'd seen a play performed by some of the actors in the ministry and, to be honest, I was a bit intimidated. Although at that time I had achieved notable career accomplishments, I was still painfully insecure so I was totally comfortable being seen and not heard.

I didn't want to make a deep commitment because, on some level, I feared not being good enough, and I had no problems letting my fear compromise the extent of my service in that ministry. Fortunately the ministry's facilitator had the discernment to see beyond my fear. She had me perform a monologue, took one look at me and told me that I was a leader and that it was futile for me to attempt to be anything less. God required my unabridged commitment and resolve and He is worthy of it.

Within weeks I was not only the lead in two productions, I was also the choreographer for every production we did. It wasn't enough for me to join the ministry, God called me to commit completely and without reservation. Fully participating in that ministry resulted in one of the most enriching seasons of my life.

Years later, God would use another life experience to teach me the beauty of commitment.

They say the first year of marriage is the hardest, filled with *I love you so much* highs and *what have I gotten myself into?* lows. It is the year you find out that you're not quite as altruistic as you thought you were and the year when you can list all of your spouse's faults verbatim while conveniently remaining blind to your own. It was during this first year that my husband and I discovered the best thing we could do for our marriage and for each other was to keep God firmly planted in the center, by coming together daily in prayer. This in no way made our marriage challenge-free but it absolutely helped to keep things in their proper perspective. Still, when two people come together to merge two very different lives into "One", those first few weeks can be a doozey! Whenever my husband and I would have the disagreements that we now lovingly refer to as our growing pains, I would get so frustrated with him that, although I never voiced it, in the back of my mind I would reminisce about the ease of being single.

Never mind that I had rolled around on the floor snotnosed and crying, melodramatically beseeching God for the blessing of marriage, and never mind that I knew without a shadow of a doubt that God had blessed me with the best man for me—the hurt, discomfort and exasperation of those early disagreements made me miss being single, where compromise and patience were seldom on the menu. The truth is, and there is no way around this, in those first months I wasn't fully committed to my marriage. Although I had no plans of leaving (ever), the fact that I was glamorizing the very singleness I had begged the Lord to relieve me of was evidence of my fear of complete, uncompromising commitment. It's funny, you take those vows, and in minutes, you become a co-member of a life-changing institution that will inevitably ask more of both of you than you initially have the selflessness to give. But unaware, you say, "I do" and through the trials of marriage, God begins to grow both of you…into your vows. Because what they don't tell you is this: You are married in an instant but you become "One" over time. And becoming "One" requires dogged commitment—commitment to work through things no matter how angry or frustrated you are, commitment to be fully known, insecurities and all, and, most important, commitment to be patient with the process while God grows and stretches both of you over time.

When we began praying daily as a couple, and when I determined to be committed not only in my actions but also in my thought life, God blessed my marriage in ways that amazed me.

In The Second Revelation, our hero struggles with his fear of vulnerability and trust. He fears needing love and being affected by it. But this is sin and folly. You can never truly experience anything unless you fully commit to it and allow it to have an affect on you. The best in life and love comes from unabashed commitment, the temerity to make a decision that requires all of you and the boldness to receive the result.

In the book of Revelations 3:15-16 the word of God says:

I know you well, you are neither hot nor cold; I wish you were one or the other! But since you are merely lukewarm, I will spit you out of my mouth.

In that scripture the Lord is admonishing the Church of Laodicea about making a firm decision and fully committing to the things of God.

The creator of the universe has not called us to be spiritual cowards. In fact quite the opposite; He has called us to be intrepid, to trust without seeing and to believe without proof. Miracles manifest when commitment abounds.

Grand commitments change the world and personal commitments reshape our lives. Each has equal value and each requires the faith of discipline and dedication. Martin Luther King Jr. decided that curing America of the inhumanity of segregation was worth making a lifetime commitment to, and as a result, forty years later, the election of America's first African American president came to pass. Every day teachers in less-than-stellar circumstances, making less-than-stellar pay, commit to sowing knowledge and values into the lives of our children and, by doing so, provide hope for our future. President John Fitzgerald Kennedy committed to sending a man to the moon and subsequently changed what the entire world viewed as possible.

Every day someone makes a commitment to change their eating habits, become more physically fit or say no to a serious addiction, and as a result, their overall health improves, they extend their lives and they serve as an inspiration to others. It has been said that great men and great women commit, but that is untrue. Greatness is that which is born out of the steady unwavering commitment of everyday men and women.

SECOND REVELATION

Journal Questions

1) What opportunity are you missing out on, or what area in your life are you not getting the most out of, because you have not made the commitment that you need to make? Why haven't you made the commitment?

_____

_____

_____

_____

_____

_____

_____

_____

_____

_____

_____

_____

_____

_____

_____

_____

_____

_____

_____

2) In regard to your answer to question number one: List five things you believe you are missing out on because you have not made the commitment.

_____
_____
_____
_____
_____
_____
_____
_____
_____
_____
_____
_____
_____
_____
_____
_____
_____
_____
_____
_____
_____
_____
_____
_____
_____
_____
_____
_____

3) Now list five positive things that could happen if
you were to follow through and fully commit.

_____

_____

_____

_____

_____

_____

_____

_____

_____

_____

_____

_____

_____

_____

_____

_____

_____

_____

_____

_____

_____

_____

_____

_____

_____

_____

_____

4) For the next five to ten minutes sit and visualize the five positive things from your list. See yourself making the commitment and see each of the five positive outcomes unfolding in your life one by one. Allow yourself to feel the excitement and the relief of attaining these goals. After you complete this visualization exercise write this statement in your journal: *Anything is possible when I commit.*

5) When in your life did you make a firm commitment and see it all the way through? How did it make you feel? Who was blessed by it and how did your life benefit as a result?

_____

_____

_____

_____

_____

_____

_____

_____

_____

_____

_____

_____

_____

_____

_____

_____

_____

_____

_____

_____

_____

_____

_____

6) Recall a time in your past when you let fear keep you from the blessing of truly committing to something and reaping the benefits of it. If you could go back in time, what advice and encouragement would you give yourself in that circumstance? What would you tell yourself to alleviate your fears?

SECOND REVELATION

Challenge

Make a commitment to what you revealed you were having trouble committing to in question number one. Remember, God meets us exactly where we are; we just have to take that initial step forward. It's time for you to be intrepid in an area of your life where you have been lukewarm by committing to something or someone completely and without fear. Be GREAT this week. Courage begins with a decision.

SECOND REVELATION

Growth Check

At this point you should have completed **The Second Revelation Questions** as well as your **Second Revelation Challenge**. Take some time to write in your journal about your experience. Or take some time to quietly reflect on the following questions:

Now that you have stepped out on faith and have fully committed, what things have you changed in your life in order to accommodate this new stance?

How has this new commitment affected you?

What challenges or benefits have come into your life as a result?

As you take this journey it is important to be cognizant of your growth, and your feelings. If you are taking this journey alone, always take the time to pray and write about your progress. If you are taking this journey within the boundaries of a group of people who are also reading The Dunes, *it is important to pray as a group as well as to share your feelings and progress with each other.*

Let's move forward in our commitment, as we embrace The Third Revelation and peel off yet another layer!

THE THIRD REVELATION

PERSEVERE

"Pretty" grows on trees like a grape in a vineyard.
But "Beauty" like wine develops over time through
the crushing of what was and the conversion of what
remains to create a sweet new beginning.

*A*s *The Other* again embarked upon the journey, she noticed that each step brought less pain than the last. The challenge of the journey had given birth to resilience, and as she examined her body, she barely recognized herself. The journey had transformed her, made her strong. Her frame, once frail and slight, was now shapely, firm and tight. *The Other* looked at herself with new eyes—God's eyes—and she discovered she wasn't dirty from head to toe after all, but rather quite the opposite. She was beautiful and compelling, *a sparkling diamond*. Excited, *The Other* let go of the rope and picked up her pace.

The Other: *I will bless him! I know who I am and I know my worth! My love will give him the wings to love without fear.*

Giddy with the thought of their union, *The Other* began running. The hot sand had become merely a spring board for her resolve, and she arrived at the top of The Dunes in record speed. Excited to share her new body and renewed spirit with him, *The Other* sought him out.

The Other: *My love, I'm here now! I'm here. I finally made it to the top! Where are you? You're not going to believe your eyes! Come see! Come see what the Lord has done!*

But there was no sign of *The One* and no answer to her calls.

So she sat and waited.

Sat and hoped.

Sat and prayed.

Sat and cried for 57 days until finally *The Other* accepted the truth: *The One* **had chosen not to love her because his limitations had a greater effect on him than she did.**

The Other staggered at the realization. Her mind flooded with the death of her hope. What now? What now!

Then, in her spirit, *The Other* heard a still small voice say: *Let your faith rest not in your own wisdom but in the power of God.*

As *The Other* received this message and believed, so began her healing. *The Other* ventured back down the hill , content to trust God for a new beginning and a love not grounded in fear.

THIRD REVELATION

Commentary

*H*ow do you handle disappointment? How do you react when you've been working on the computer for hours and your document, for whatever reason, gets deleted and all of your hard work is now in vain? How do you feel when you've sowed seeds in earnest for months, maybe even years, with the expectation of a favorable outcome only to have the desired result put off once again? How do you handle it when you've waited faithfully, prayed and trusted God for a new chapter to open up in your life, only to find yourself back at square one? What do you do? Do you give up? Do you temporarily divorce God? After all, doesn't He see how hard you're trying? Why doesn't He do something to help you out?

As I pen this, I struggle with severe discoloration on my face as a result of a beauty product that had a negative effect on my skin. I have dealt with this for over a year; it is hideous and I hate it. I have spent hundreds of dollars, maybe even close to a few thousand, on skin peels and creams in an effort to correct it but it has all been to no avail and I hate it. I want my face back! I want to stop wearing a pound of makeup every day in an effort to hide it. I want to stop feeling self-conscious and ugly. I want to be healed. I want to look in the faces of family members, friends and strangers and not see the look in their eyes as they notice it and try valiantly (bless their hearts) not to focus on it and continue in conversation. Did I mention that I hate it!

Every morning I fight feelings of dread and intense shame before I summon up the courage to look at myself in the mirror. Every morning I pray (sometimes in tears) and remind myself that it won't always be like this. I will heal. Every morning I try to suppress the overwhelming humiliation of feeling unattractive in front of my husband and every morning he does everything in his power to let me know that those thoughts are in my head alone. At one point, it got so bad that I literally dreamed about my skin and how desperately I want God to heal me. But He hasn't yet, and every morning it breaks my heart.

Still, I have made the decision that one day He will heal me, so every morning I get over myself, take a deep breath and choose to enjoy my husband, my family, my friends and my life in spite of my hope deferred. Because even though I don't see Him in this, I know that He sees me and, though He tarries, in faith I will wait.

There comes a time in every believer's life when he or she will feel Godforsaken. I know at just this moment there are readers "rebuking" and "binding" my words. Yet the truth remains: There are times in life when you will feel pain with no immediate relief and despair with no immediate solution. And although I know character and a deeper understanding of Christ are born through trials and tribulation, I do not wish them on anyone. But if even our Lord and Savior found himself at a moment in his humanity where he felt Godforsaken, why would we be exempt?

I now speak to those who at one time or another have felt like God has forgotten about them.

As a Christian, you followed the formula. You prayed, obeyed, trusted and waited but still…He didn't show. You saw friends blessed. You witnessed family members overcome obstacles. You even shouted and praised at the manifestation of other folks' miracles. But for you, no breakthrough. It didn't happen. It almost seemed personal. "Why not me, God?" or "Why is this happening to me, God?"

Trust me, if you live long enough, you will ask a version of this question. There are times in our journey when we will grapple between faith and despair, our hearts permeating heaven with a deafening yell..."Where are you?! My parent is dying. My loved one is sick. I have no money. I am all alone. I can't find work. I am persecuted, beaten, abused, abandoned...Where are you?!"

Author and poet Maya Angelou poignantly wrote:

"Someone was hurt before you; wronged before you, hungry before you, frightened before you, beaten before you; humiliated before you, raped before you... yet, someone survived...You can do anything you choose to do."

And that is where we find ourselves, littered with the scars of our battle, facing a choice. God didn't show up and do the thing you hoped He would. There was no healing, no breakthrough, no miracle and no rescue...so what now?

> *We are pressed on every side by troubles, but we*
> *are not crushed; we are perplexed but not driven*
> *to despair. We are hunted down, but never aban-*
> *doned by God. We get knocked down but we are not*
> *destroyed. -2Corinthians 4:8-9*

Your heart's desire did not manifest like you wanted it to; in fact, you don't know if it ever will, but by the grace of God, there are still other things in your life to rejoice about, and this, quite frankly, is where true Christian maturity begins. This is the moment that separates the babes from the grown-ups. Are you going to become stronger and wiser because of your experience or are you going to be defeated by it?

No one looks forward to a trial, me included. No one wants to reach rock bottom in any area of life, nor have their hopes and dreams deferred. No one desires to lose a loved one to a heinous disease or a tragic crime. But the truth is sometimes bad circumstances occur in the lives of good people, they just do, and it is in these happenings that we discover more of who God truly is. I would have never known Him as a healer if I hadn't been sick or if my spirit hadn't been broken. I would have never known Him as a provider if I hadn't been down to my last dime. And I would have never known that He placed inside me the strength to overcome if He rescued me from every trial.

Triumph over past pain comes not only from discovering who God is but also from the ability to give the gift of forgiveness.

The primary beneficiary of this gift is not the person you need to forgive or the situation you need to make peace with. The primary beneficiary of forgiveness is you. This is a spiritual and a scientific fact. When we are able to forgive, it is cleansing and healing to our bodies as well as our souls. When we do not forgive, our bodies hold on to toxins and negative thought patterns that have a detrimental effect on our whole being.

But how do we forgive? How do we make peace?

There is no perfect formula or process, especially when the affront is egregious. Every situation like every person is different. The beginning of forgiveness, as with everything, is prayer. And although each path to forgiveness is as different as the offense, there are certain steps that will lead you on your way. Whatever was done, despite whoever did it, you must first learn to accept it. Rehearsing it over and over again in your mind, or lamenting about how you wish things had turned out differently, is never going to change what happened. As painful as it may be, it happened, accept it.

Acceptance does not mean that you have to be okay with what happened. It means that you understand fully that your power does not exist in the past to change it; your power exists in the present to overcome it. Acceptance enables you to move forward and create reasonable expectations, to establish boundaries through heartfelt discussions and to make the decisions you need to make regarding your own life.

Boundaries should never be motivated by fear. Fear is not a part of forgiveness nor is it a part of making peace with the past. Healthy boundaries are motivated by wisdom gained through the experience and gained through prayer.

Finally, release it. Though it is easy to say and much harder to do, give it to God and let it go. It is the past, it is over and it only has the power you attach to it. You honor no one's memory by spending the rest of your life miserable, angry or bitter. You do not enact justice by shrinking and becoming a shell of who God created you to be. You enact justice when you flourish and forgive in spite of what happened.

Several years ago I toured in a Christian play entitled *S.T.E.M.* It was a theatrical ministry vehicle I co-wrote with three of my dearest friends. It was composed of dramatic and comedic monologues where we would give our personal testimonies of how, by grace, we not only survived things like molestation, rape and domestic abuse but triumphed through the power of forgiveness and faith. Our testimonies and our witness of God's faithfulness encouraged women in similar circumstances to persevere, to have hope and expectancy in a God who is able to bring us through.

It is one of the many purposes of the Body of Christ to be a refuge in the storm and a light at the end of the tunnel. After each play, we were thronged by women, who were weeping and grateful that we had shared our stories of pain, disappointment and triumph with them. Not only because they could identify with them but because they saw that they were not alone and, just like us, they could overcome. The word of God says: *We are saved by the blood of the lamb and the word of our testimony.*

Sometimes God will not spare us from a painful experience. Sometimes we are going to go through something awful and emerge with an inner strength that we never knew we had. Use what you learn during those seasons to be a blessing to others. That is the kingdom of Heaven.

THIRD REVELATION

Journal Questions

1) What hurt or disappointment in your life has so deeply affected you that it is robbing you of joy and peace? What has dealing with this life experience revealed to you about yourself?

_____

_____

_____

_____

_____

_____

_____

_____

_____

_____

_____

_____

_____

_____

_____

_____

_____

_____

_____

_____

_____

_____

2) Oftentimes residual hurt or anger is an indication that we have not forgiven the person or made peace with the situation that caused it. Why do you believe you have not been able to forgive or make peace?

_____

_____

_____

_____

_____

_____

_____

_____

_____

_____

_____

_____

_____

_____

_____

_____

_____

_____

_____

_____

_____

_____

_____

3) **Who in your life has offered you forgiveness? What effect did this generosity of spirit have on your life?**

_____

_____

_____

_____

_____

_____

_____

_____

_____

_____

_____

_____

_____

_____

_____

_____

_____

_____

_____

_____

_____

_____

_____

_____

_____

_____

_____

_____

4) *Let's play a game! In this game you get to be your own parent. Picture yourself as a child—much like the one in The First Revelation—in a beautiful lush garden surrounded by all that you will ever need. Now picture yourself (the child) sitting at the edge of the garden, head down, alone, nursing a wound. As the parent you are going* to *lovingly convince the child (yourself) to take part in the fullness of the garden. Read the following dialogue and then finish the scenario with the parental response.*

Parent: Why are you sitting here alone and sad?

Child: I got hurt when I was playing in the garden so I've decided that I don't want to play anymore. It's not fair! None of the other kids got hurt like this. Besides, it would be too painful and embarrassing to play again.

Parent: I love you and I am so sorry you got hurt but I can promise you two things. One, there is more to the garden than the pain you experienced. Two, you will never know all there is if you don't play again.

Child: But it really hurts! And I don't understand why this happened to me...I don't think I will ever be able to play the same again.

Your turn! Take some time to comfort the child. Then encourage the child with all of the reasons he/she should explore the garden and play again.

Parent:

_____
_____
_____
_____
_____
_____
_____
_____
_____
_____
_____
_____
_____
_____
_____
_____
_____
_____
_____
_____
_____
_____
_____
_____
_____
_____
_____
_____
_____
_____

5) Who in your life has used what they have learned
from past experiences of pain or disappointment
to bless you? How can you use what you have
learned in your season of hurt or disappointment
to bless others?

_____

_____

_____

_____

_____

_____

_____

_____

_____

_____

_____

_____

_____

_____

_____

_____

_____

_____

_____

_____

_____

_____

_____

_____

THIRD REVELATION

Challenge

Forgive. Forgive the person or circumstance that caused your hurt or disappointment. Forgive. Forgive the person who cut you off in traffic. Forgive your boss or co-worker. Forgive the person who broke your heart. Forgive yourself for making the mistake that you thought you were too smart to make. Forgive. Forgive your friend for saying that thing that really hurt and offended you. Forgive. Stop being angry at God for the pain of the past or for what hasn't manifested in your life yet and thank Him for all of the good in your life because it is only by His mercy and grace that you are still here. Forgive and let go. Do not let anything continue to rob you of the joy of what's to come. Forgive, so that you may fully receive. Forgive, and indulge in the freedom, power and healing that comes from it.

THIRD REVELATION

Growth Check

At this point you should have completed **The Third Revelation Questions** as well as your **Third Revelation Challenge**. Take some time to write in your journal about your experience. Or take some time to quietly reflect on the following comments and questions:

In The First and Second Revelations we learn the blessing of releasing fear and fully committing through faith. In The Third Revelation we seek to live life in all of its fullness by letting go of the past through forgiveness.

Forgiveness is sometimes a process done over time through prayer and an act of your will. If you were not able to immediately forgive an egregious offense don't worry. As I said, it is a process. Begin with an earnest desire to forgive and, in time, as you remain prayerful and willing, the Lord will lead your heart into full forgiveness.

What benefits are you looking forward to when you are able to fully forgive?

What blessings have come into your life in the areas in which you were able to offer immediate forgiveness?

As you take this journey it is important to be cognizant of your growth, and your feelings. If you are taking this journey alone, always take the time to pray and write about your progress. If you are taking this journey within the boundaries of a group of people who are also reading The Dunes, *it is important to pray as a group as well as to share your feelings and progress with each other.*

Let's continue our growth as we journey on to The Fourth Revelation!

THE FOURTH REVELATION

TRUST

*Trust is not found in that glorious moment of hope
where the best is envisioned on the other side. But
instead in that awkward moment of obedience when
fear surrounds and logic yells, "Fool!" Yet, standing
in the dark, seeing nothing...you still follow Him.*

he Other arrived at the bottom of The Dunes convinced their story was over and that her destiny would now be paired with another. She examined her feet, and to *The Other's* delight, they had become quite splendid from the journey, tanned and golden, yet soft to the touch. She reached down to dust off the sand.

The One: *The man I was could not truly receive you. The man I've become refuses to live without you.*

The Other looked up and, to her surprise, there he was, her love. He was even more handsome than she had remembered. He stood magnificent, facing her at the bottom of the hill.

She stammered in confusion...........

The Other: *But you weren't there. I waited for you.*

He smiled, delighting in the beauty of her heart.

The Other: *I waited for days, but you never came.*

The One: *I came when God told me I was ready. The truth is I'm right on time.*

Her mind raced a mile a minute. The sound of her heart pounded through her chest.

The Other: *But I thought you didn't..........*

The One: *You were wrong.*

The Other: *You mean you still.........*

The One: *Never stopped.*

The Other: *But all this time...all the distance.*

The One: *Was worked according to our good.*

The One had made it down the hill before she got there. He knew that truly receiving her meant not leaning to that which was familiar, but instead trusting God. So he left behind what was and made a choice to cleave to what would be. *The Other* was astounded. *The One* actually made it down the hill! He tackled his dune! Her worries and resolutions were now meaningless in the face of God's divine plan. Then *The Other* remembered the words of the still small voice…*Let your faith rest not in your own wisdom but in the power of God.*

The Other: *I don't know what to say.*

He smiled.

The One: *I do.*

The One took *The Other* in his arms and kissed every fear away. He promised life and they both believed it.

FOURTH REVELATION

Commentary

I have always believed that the two greatest gifts in life are love and flourishing in a career or a calling that you are passionate about. I can still hear Billy Dee Williams' character in the 1975 romantic motion picture *Mahogany* say the words that echoed in the heart of every movie-goer in the theatre, as we stumbled along with Diana Ross's character to compose ourselves under the weight of their poignancy: "Success is nothing, without someone you love to share it with." I was a little girl when I saw that movie. Still, in that moment, I understood fully that , for me, it had to be both: love and career fulfillment.

Which is precisely why, as I approached my fortieth birthday and had achieved neither, I felt like an utter failure. Sure, outside of a successful career and love, there were other things I would have been delighted to wake up to on my birthday...beautiful surroundings, a great hair day and a scale that read my dream weight no matter what I ate. Any of those things would have been high on my list. Waking up forty, single and broke in Los Angeles was not.

But, like it or not, that's where I found myself days before my fortieth birthday, the birthday I had decided I was not, under any circumstances, going to celebrate. The conversation with my best friend went a little something like this: "What is there to celebrate? I mean I am grateful to be alive but the last thing I want to do is celebrate. I'm middle aged, single and so financially strapped that I had to move back in with my mother. My life has become a cautionary tale of what not to do." She paused (because after years of friendship we knew how to deal with each other's drama-queen moments) and said, "Erin, if you don't celebrate, you will look back on that decision and regret it. Things aren't going the way you want them to, but that shouldn't stop you from celebrating this milestone in your life. Forty is a milestone! You made it and it's worth celebrating."

I thought about what she said long and hard. My life absolutely didn't look like I expected it to look at the age of forty, but she was right. That didn't mean life wasn't worth celebrating and that the milestone wasn't worth recognizing. So I called fifteen of my closest girlfriends (who were all married with kids and in desperate need of a girls' get-away weekend), and we caravanned to Vegas where I brought in my fortieth birthday surrounded by love, friends and fun.

Our first night in Vegas, we hung out in our hotel lobby, where a DJ played and we danced until dawn. Somewhere in between the picture taking, the laughter and the fun, I looked around at my girlfriends, who I had known since my twenties. I was healthy, I was having the time of my life and I was with people who loved and celebrated me. No matter what disappointments I had, life was still worth celebrating—God was opening my eyes and changing my mind.

When I got back home from Vegas, I determined to trust God in a way I hadn't before. In the past when I believed in something with all of my heart and it hadn't come to pass, I was devastated. At forty and forward, that was no longer going to be my mantra.

At ages thirty-eight and thirty-nine the thought of turning forty still single and broke was like death. Well, that's exactly what happened, and although I may have felt like dying, my body (Thank God!) was healthy, and I had no plans of accommodating my self-pity, so it was obvious I needed a new plan. I decided to not only trust God for my heart's desire but to trust His heart and His sovereign desire. It would be the greatest balancing act of my life: I would believe and let go all at the same time. I would stand in faith for what I hoped for, but if it did not come to pass, I would continue to trust God and trust the unfolding of His plan, whatever it was.

I made the decision to be happy and enjoy my life however it unfolded but until the fat lady sang I was going to confess with my mouth and believe with my heart for marriage and career fulfillment. I began using the gifts God gave me by starting an online thought leader's forum on the latest political hot topics. I produced and hosted an online show featuring panel discussions on emerging social issues designed to engage, expose and enlighten. In fact it was at one of the forums that an acquaintance, who I had invited to be part of a panel, took me aside and asked me whether I was open to meeting a friend of hers. I said yes and two years later, her friend became my husband.

Our wedding was a dream come true. It was perfect in every way, and the very presence of God was felt throughout the day. The acquaintance who had introduced us, who was by now my beloved friend, sang at our wedding, and her husband performed the ceremony. I was married at forty-two but when it happened it was with the absolute right person at the absolute right time for us. God is faithful and He knows what He is doing.

At the age of thirty-nine I thought all was lost. Then God opened my eyes and I decided to believe that all was waiting for me just around the bend. Putting my complete trust in God literally transformed my life. It opened the door to love, purpose and family.

Webster's Dictionary defines *providence* as a noun, meaning *showing prudent forethought; divine protection and guidance.*

The providence of God is unfailing. The manifestation and timing of my marriage is just one of the ways in which God has shown me His divine providence. *For everything there is a season, a divine purpose for everything under the sun.*

In chapters thirty-seven through fifty of the book of Genesis we learn the story of Joseph. Much like *The One* in our story, God reveals His purpose for Joseph's life before Joseph is spiritually mature enough to receive it. Joseph sees in a dream that one day he will be a ruler of many. When Joseph has the dream he is a boy. However, he is not truly able to walk in that promise until he is a man. God allows Joseph to be betrayed, falsely accused and imprisoned before Joseph is spiritually mature enough to receive all that God has for him. If we were to look at Joseph's life while he was lying in his prison bed, we might foolishly think that he was never going to amount to anything. However, Joseph becomes a wise and respected leader in Egypt, second only to the king.

In The Fourth Revelation we read that *The Other* didn't see God working on her heart's desire, so she assumed it had escaped her. She was wrong. God was preparing it so that it would be perfectly suited for her. God is the alpha and the omega. He sees the beginning and the end. He knows how to cultivate the middle for our good. She didn't need to work or strive. Her heart's desire and her destiny were given to her by the grace of a loving, omniscient, omnipresent, providential God.

Many times in life we put God on our time table. We fence Him in with our finite minds and limited understanding. But our miracles are not based on the scope of our reasoning and abilities. If they were, they wouldn't be miracles. They would be our creations. Our miracles are based on a limitless, infinite God who is able to do an exceeding and abundant work in our lives. In our story, it is significant that *The One* made it down the hill before she did; it is an illustration of the sovereignty and providence of God. HE knows what you need before you need it and prepares it for you at just the right time.

> *I had fainted, unless I had believed to see the goodness*
> *of the Lord in the land of the living. Wait on the Lord:*
> *be of good courage, and he shall strengthen your heart:*
> *wait, I say, on the Lord.* –Psalm 27:13-14

FOURTH REVELATION

Journal Questions

1) What hope or dream have you lost faith in? Why has it become a challenge for you to trust God in this area of your life?

_____
_____
_____
_____
_____
_____
_____
_____
_____
_____
_____
_____
_____
_____
_____
_____
_____
_____
_____
_____
_____
_____

2) Let's examine your inner dialogue regarding this hope or dream. Take a moment to be still and clear your mind. When you are in a place of peace, reflect on this hope or dream. Write down any fears or negative thoughts that come into your mind within the first few moments.

_____
_____
_____
_____
_____
_____
_____
_____
_____
_____
_____
_____
_____
_____
_____
_____
_____
_____
_____
_____
_____
_____

3) **Now, for every negative thought you listed, write a positive, faith-filled affirmation.**

For example:

(Negative thought) *It's too late for me to go back to school and get a degree. I am too old and I would just end up looking like an out-of-date fool.*

(Positive affirmation) *It is never too late to learn new things or expand and grow my mind. God is the author of my destiny, and as long as I am still here, there is still time.*

THE DUNES

4) Obedience is also an expression of faith. What area of your life have you not submitted in total obedience to God? What would it look like to trust God in this area? What would you have to change or do differently?

But without faith it is impossible to please Him;
for he that cometh to God must believe that He
exists, and that He is a rewarder of those that
diligently seek Him. -Hebrews 11:6

5) **List five instances in your lifetime where what you hoped for, believed in or had faith in actually manifested.** The examples don't need to be out-of-this-world miraculous. They just need to be five instances where a sincere hope of your heart manifested into a tangible result.

_____

_____

_____

_____

_____

_____

_____

_____

_____

_____

_____

_____

_____

_____

_____

_____

_____

_____

_____

_____

JOURNAL QUESTIONS

FOURTH REVELATION

Challenge

For The Fourth Revelation Challenge, you can either do Challenge A or Challenge B, or if you are feeling especially faith filled you can do BOTH.

CHALLENGE A

Trust God with that secret dream you gave up on. Believe again! Every time a negative thought pops up, combat it with a positive affirmation. It's time for the balancing act of your life!

Sow some seeds into your desired goal but at the same time release it and allow God to revive or reconstruct your dream to His good pleasure.

CHALLENGE B

Trust God in an area of your life where you have been doing things "your way" and have consistently ended up getting the same results. Obedience to His word is the key to unlock the door to His blessings. It's time to trust God completely and let Christ truly be Lord of your life in every aspect.

FOURTH REVELATION

Growth Check

At this point you should have completed **The Fourth Revelation Questions** as well as begun your **Fourth Revelation Challenge**. Take some time to write in your journal about your experience. Or take a moment to quietly reflect on the following comments and questions:

We have begun to tackle our fears, stepped out and made a bold commitment as well as moved forward in forgiveness. However, none of these things will give you the fullness of life you seek without you putting your complete and utter trust in God.

In The Fourth Revelation Challenge we made a commitment to dream again and to trust God in an area of our lives that we had never truly surrendered to Him.

One is your heart's desire. The other is your walk in righteousness. Both require faith and neither can be accomplished without fully surrendering to the Holy Spirit.

In these next few pages, journal about your new day-to-day experience of trusting God in one or both of these areas.

As you take this journey it is important to be cognizant of your growth, and your feelings. If you are taking this journey alone, always take the time to pray and write about your progress. If you are taking this journey within the boundaries of a group of people who are also reading The Dunes *it is important to pray as a group as well as to share your feelings and progress with each other.*

We've come too far to turn back now! Let's dive right in to The Fifth Revelation!

THE FIFTH REVELATION

GRACE

Christ…the perfect example,
love…the truest mirror,
humanity…the flawed vessel,
and in this we find our journey.

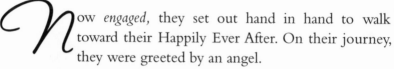

*N*ow *engaged,* they set out hand in hand to walk toward their Happily Ever After. On their journey, they were greeted by an angel.

Angel: God has smiled on you and I have come to remind you through His word that which is important, lest you fall prey to the snares of the enemy.

The couple was incredulous. They had waited so long for love. Their faith had already been tested, so how could they possibly fall into a trap? But they were gracious in *their* righteousness and listened anyway.

Angel: The book of life has one author, yet it was written by many servants. Luke was one of them. In his book, chapter ten verses thirty-eight through forty-two, he recounts the story of when Christ visits Mary and Martha. It is an illustration of the importance of perspective and priority. As soon as our Lord entered their home, he began to lovingly teach and preach the gospel. Mary, knowing the value of what was in front of her, immediately sat at our Lord's feet, listening intently to all he shared.

Now, Martha's actions were commendable but also unwise. She did not place value on the intimate and immediate presence of Christ but rather on the external preparation of his arrival. Her mistake was not in her concern for showing hospitality, because she was motivated to do so out of a sincere love for our Lord. Her mistake was in her obsession with it. She was so worried about everything that needed to be done, she became distracted by it.

Good stewardship over what God has provided is commendable but worry and distraction is sin and folly when it takes you away from the source of your provision. Martha should have been with her sister at the feet of Christ, receiving without distraction that which is priceless.

Truly I say unto you, love God, love each other and, united through prayer and purpose, tend to the cares of life. Heed this message and you will not fail.

The One: *Thank you for your words. I know what a gift she is; I will never take her nor my stewardship for granted.*

The Other: *He is a blessing. My patience will never leave him and I will trust God to guide our love in every way.*

And so the couple bid the angel farewell and went off to make the exact mistakes they had sworn not to make. Then one day *The One* looked up, and sadly, *The Other* was gone.

And that is where we find them...

———

The One was livid.

The One: *I'm tired of trying and tired of failing. I'm tired of loving and sick of loss. But most of all, I am sick of this woman! She is impatient, judgmental, dismissive and extreme!*

I'm done!

GOD: **You love *The Other*.**

The One: *I'm done!*

GOD: **You need *The Other*.**

The One: *I need air; I do not need this headache. I'm done!*

GOD: **But *The Other* is yours.**

The One: *Did anybody tell her this? Because it seems like everything she does is to show me that she is not mine! I'm done!*

GOD: **You did not ask for a woman you could live with but one you could not live without. I have given you that woman.**

The man turned to God in anger but dared not refute him.

The One: *You have also given me free will. I choose to no longer fight for our love.*

GOD: **You have** *never* **fought for this love.**

Filled with frustration *The One* slowly responded.

The One: *I have done nothing but fight for her. I have bent myself into a pretzel trying to please her. If that's not fighting, then I don't know what is.*

GOD: **Then you are right, son. You don't know what it is. When I gave you this woman my plan was complete and I rested. Neither my word nor my plan return to me void. My perfection manifests itself through imperfect vessels.**

The One: *I don't understand.*

GOD: **Well, let's look at it more closely.**

Instantly *The One* was catapulted through time. He felt as though he were floating, able to see the events of his life as if he were watching them on a grand movie screen. He witnessed the very beginning of their love when fear was the master of his heart. But as he surrendered to God he gained revelation of *The Other's* heart and overcame his limitations to reach out to her.

GOD: **I simply returned my gift to its intended recipient. Recognizing my truth and accepting what I have for you is not fighting.**

In a flash, he watched himself and *The Other* face their most recent challenges. *The One* realized that although love abounded in his heart, it did not always manifest in his actions. And so their love struggled with a series of ups and downs, all requiring a level of transparency that was new to him.

GOD: Extending yourself in a love that has been divinely set before you is not fighting. Initially you marveled at my gift, excited about the endless possibilities. But as the cares of life set in, instead of using my gift for its intended purpose—to have *The Other* **as your partner, your confidante and your comfort—you chose to toil on your own, neglecting my purpose and forsaking your stewardship. There are things I designed for the two of you to glean from each other, but your emotional isolation and her fear made this impossible.**

The One: *She left me!*

GOD: No, she left the hurt and the frustration.

Transported again the man saw their love. *The Other's* exit, like a thief in the night, came as a painful shock. That which *The One* feared most had come upon him. She abandoned him. The memory and the pain coursed fresh through his veins. Rife with anger and defiance, he rebutted the Lord…

The One: *How can I possibly fight if she gives up?!*

GOD: My son, as a sports enthusiast you know the difference between *playing to win* **and** *playing not to lose.*

When you truly fight, you give your best, your all. You stand boldly and fearlessly no matter what the opposition, no matter what the cost. In this effort you are *playing to win.* **And as my spirit works in you, victory is assured. But when your constant concern is giving too much, losing ground or being taken advantage of, you are** *playing not to lose.* **And surely, inevitably, you will. I have created within you a warrior, yet you constantly let fear subdue you, and**

become virtually defeated by choice. You arrive to the fight and step into the ring, but your pride never lets you leave the corner.

No, son, unfortunately for this love you have not fought.

Pierced by the two edged sword, perspective engulfed him. Although he had stepped out of his comfort zone, he had not given his all. He had not fought for this love. Sitting alone, *The One* realized that he had not given his best and he had not heeded the angel's warning. Like Martha he had been foolishly distracted and forgotten that which was truly important.

<hr/>

Meanwhile, *The Other* was ranting…

The Other: *He is the most selfish man I have ever met! I gave and I gave; I sacrificed and I compromised, and not once did he respond in kind. All I got was a bunch of empty promises and punished for loving too much!*

I'm done!

GOD: *The One* loves you.

The Other: *Love? Love! He refuses to do even the smallest things that are needed to make me feel safe in this relationship! What kind of love is content in giving the least? I'm done!*

GOD: Providing for you is foremost in his heart.

The Other: *Really? Then why don't I know or feel that?! Love is not a secret! You give it and you profess it, but he was more concerned with appearing not to need me, than with recognizing the need we have for each other. Father, really…I'm done!*

GOD: Only with *The One* has your soul felt truly content.

The Other: *And only with* The One *have I been in a relationship and yet at times felt utterly alone.*

GOD: **You did not ask for a buddy. You asked for a leader, a provider and a visionary. I have given you that man.**

Then *The Other* remembered her secret prayer to God, when she asked Him to bless her with a covering, a leader, a provider and a visionary. She laughed to herself. She had forgotten to ask that her mate cherish her.

The Other: *Father, indeed you did bless me with a visionary and in that he is resolute. He is disciplined and purposed in every way, but he is not yet a leader and I was not cherished. Now I realize how much I need that as well.*

GOD: **And who have you been created to cherish?**

The Other: *The man you gave me to.*

GOD: **No. You have been purposed to be a companion to the man. You have been created to cherish me. And in that, you have failed.**

The Other recalled her relationship with *The One*. How they both carried old wounds. Since childhood, *The One* had learned to keep his feelings buried and use apathy as a form of self-protection. But that is not faith and it doesn't work in a love relationship. *The Other* thought of her own culpability, her childhood fear of abandonment. Leave before being left. Hadn't she beaten that by now? She endured so much before she walked away. Still, in the end, she left without words rather than rise to the challenge of love's occasion.

The Other: *How, Lord? How have I forsaken you?*

GOD: **Do you remember the angel's warning?**

The Other: *Yes.*

GOD: Then why didn't I find you at my feet? I have placed within you a delicacy and a truth, the perfect accent for his strength, and yet you said nothing.

The Other: *I silenced myself for fear of losing his love and approval.*

GOD: I blessed you with tongue and voice, and yet you chose not to glorify me by speaking the truth in love. Your fear was no longer in me but in *The One* I created. Your desire was to gain his approval, not mine. In seeking only to please *The One*, you shut me out. Your fear and lack of faith are an insult to my power. I am able to restore all I have divinely orchestrated. Neither my word nor my plan return to me void. Yet you acted on your fear instead of trusting in my light. Because of this, you have once again been disappointed and because of *The One's* folly, he again knows loss.

Convicted, the woman fell to her knees and prayed.

The Other: *Lord, please forgive us and shine your light that we may know your beauty and seek your face. Speak life into the love you have given and restore that which is in your will. Heal us, Father, that we may be prevailing testimonies of your grace. These things I ask in Jesus' name. Amen.*

Reconciliation would take a miracle.

FIFTH REVELATION

Commentary

*A*new commandment I give unto you, that ye love one another; as I have loved you. By this shall all men know that ye are my disciples, if ye have love one to another. (John 13:34-35)

Many times in the New Testament, Christ exhorts us to treat each other with the love and consideration He freely gives each of us. We distinguish ourselves from the rest of the world by our treatment of each other. It is how we identify ourselves as His.

Of course this is easier said than done at times. When we are fed up with a person or a situation the idea of "loving our neighbor" seems preposterous, especially if we feel we have given more than enough, or that our anger is justified. But even so, more times than not, if we distance ourselves to gain a more objective perspective, we see that we could have been more patient, more compassionate and most certainly extended more of an effort to see things through the other person's point of view. I offer myself as an example: I am very politically active; I read voraciously and I'm passionate about my views. In the past this caused me to be a bit self-righteous and tunnel-visioned. During this season the Lord saw fit to bless me with employment in a company where I worked in the field doing research for several years. I encountered many different people from many different cultures and socio-economic backgrounds. It gave me the unique opportunity to go beyond the veil, to get to know people on a three-dimensional level as full-bodied human beings who had, during the course of their lives, encountered things I had never been exposed to and who saw the world through completely different paradigms.

One day I was interviewing a woman in her home who I had grown rather fond of during the course of her participation in our research study. I found out that not only did we not share the same political beliefs or perspectives but that our views were in complete opposition. This blew my mind because in the course of getting to know her, I had felt a distinct connection with her and believed we shared a common bond. In my heart she had become my friend. So to find out that day that she held a belief system that neither I nor anybody in my circle of friends or family shared amazed me. But the even more unsettling realization was that if I was honest with myself, had I known about her beliefs beforehand, I would have written her off and never taken the time to get to know her. The awareness of my immaturity and prejudice gave me pause.

That day, instead of dismissing her in my mind as foolish and misguided, I decided to play a game with myself. While driving home in my car, I determined to argue her point of view in my mind under the guise that she may be right. The exercise allowed me to go deeper than my perspective. Equipped with a clearer picture of who she was, I had the opportunity to love a human being with whom I had very little in common. It made me realize that, at the end of the day, none of that stuff really matters. During a memorial service what is honored and remembered is not where someone stood on an issue or who they voted for, but whose lives that person blessed, who they loved and who loved them in return while they inhabited this earth.

In the same regard, love requires not only that we expand the net and open our hearts to people from every walk of life and every side of the spectrum, but also that we honor each other's God-given uniqueness and individual paths of discovery and personal growth. Everyone's journey is unique to them. Respecting our differences and learning to love each other in spite of them is one of life's great lessons. We do not all look the same, love the same or like the same things. Diversity and difference are the great gifts of humanity; learning to work together in inclusion is our great challenge.

On many occasions we try to change our family or friends or judge each other's life choices. And though our need to interfere or save someone from themselves is often motivated by love or good intentions, it is still, even in its sincerity, an attempt to navigate someone else's journey. This is especially tempting when we see loved ones making decisions that put their health in jeopardy or that rob them of time and have a detrimental effect on their overall lives. But here's the thing…until they love themselves enough to change their situation or until they have learned the life lessons that they need to learn, change will not come. You cannot force your so-called good judgment on grown people. You can give unconditional love and support to someone who is sincerely trying to change. You can share wisdom, or you can practice tough love when the situation calls for it but you cannot bring the change about for them. Period.

There comes a time when, even as a parent, you have to step back and let your children learn some of life's hard lessons. Likewise there comes a time when, as a friend or a loved one, you must recognize that everyone is entitled to their own life journey. Everyone is entitled to their very own successes, failures, mistakes, loves and lessons. Their journey is not yours to navigate, control or determine. We cannot sit in the driver's seat of any life but our own. Stop trying to save fish from drowning. Trust me, you will be happier. Life is built for joy and heart break, success and failure, love and loss. Just as no two finger prints are alike, neither are our life journeys. Give others the gift that God has given you, the free will to create, explore and make your own path, mistakes and all. Trust that He will find them, just as He found you, with an unfailing love and a flawless navigation.

FIFTH REVELATION

Journal Questions

1) What relationship or circumstance have you fallen short in extending the love, patience and grace of God? Provide a detailed example.

_____
_____
_____
_____
_____
_____
_____
_____
_____
_____
_____
_____
_____
_____
_____
_____
_____
_____
_____
_____
_____
_____

2) Still thinking of this same relationship or circumstance, what things can you now begin to do to be a better example of the grace and mercy of Christ?

_____

_____

_____

_____

_____

_____

_____

_____

_____

_____

_____

_____

_____

_____

_____

_____

_____

_____

_____

_____

_____

_____

_____

_____

_____

_____

3) Think of a time in your life when someone extended the patience, love and grace of Christ to you. It could be a time when someone let you take your time in repaying a debt. Or maybe it was when someone stood by your side through a painful ordeal. How did this generosity of spirit make you feel? What weight was lifted as a result?

_____

_____

_____

_____

_____

_____

_____

_____

_____

_____

_____

_____

_____

_____

_____

_____

_____

_____

_____

_____

FIFTH REVELATION

Challenge

Do something for someone other than yourself. Say yes instead of saying no. Give of yourself in a sacrificial way. Sometimes the best gift you can give someone is your undivided time and attention so give it freely and with reckless abandon. There are many non-profit organizations that need weekend volunteers. Seek one out and volunteer your time. There are many seniors who would love a helping hand or someone to talk to. Visit a senior center and see if you can be of service. Whether you choose a family member, a friend or a perfect stranger, extend yourself to someone and be a blessing. When you make a difference in someone's day, you have made a difference in someone's life.

FIFTH REVELATION

Growth Check

At this point you should have completed **The Fifth Revelation Questions** as well as your **Fifth Revelation Challenge**. Take some time to write in your journal about your experience. Or take a moment to quietly reflect on the following comments and questions:

You have now embarked on a journey of sowing the seeds of boldness, commitment, forgiveness, trust and, now, generosity of spirit. The harvest of these virtues is priceless.

In The Fifth Revelation Challenge you were asked to give of yourself sacrificially. It has been said that there is more joy in giving than receiving.

Journal about your experiences in giving: Who did you bless and how did it make you feel to do it?

As you take this journey it is important to be cognizant of your growth, and your feelings. If you are taking this journey alone, always take the time to pray and write about your progress. If you are taking this journey within the boundaries of a group of people who are also reading The Dunes, *it is important to pray as a group as well as to share your feelings and progress with each other.*

Just look at you. You have a glow you didn't have back during that First Revelation! Let's add some more radiance to that shine and journey on to The Sixth Revelation.

THE SIXTH REVELATION

SURRENDER

Surrender is…basking in the refuge of an unlimited God while clothed in the confines of your humanity.

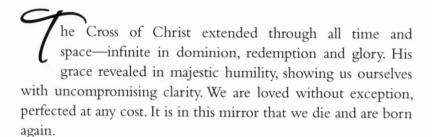

*T*he Cross of Christ extended through all time and space—infinite in dominion, redemption and glory. His grace revealed in majestic humility, showing us ourselves with uncompromising clarity. We are loved without exception, perfected at any cost. It is in this mirror that we die and are born again.

───•◦•───

The Other's days without *The One* were mute and desolate. A shell of herself, she went through the motions, wondering whether her soul could bear another moment of his absence. *The Other* found that her joy was inextricably tied to him, and now that their relationship had unraveled her sadness knew no cure. Every crime *The Other* had charged him with, she now stood parallel in guilt. Treating that which is precious as if it were common—as *The Other* stood in the light of the Cross—she saw her reflection and was ashamed.

The Other: *I understand now that to love unconditionally is also to trust without condition, to abide in earnest faithfulness, seeing first your beloved's heart over any hurt or offense.*

Oh the joy and angst of divine providence. Her role had been revealed, to speak the truth with the steadfastness of a friend, and to love with the tenderness of a lifetime confidante. And in all occasions, trust Him whose plan had brought them together in the first place. In the mercy of the Cross, she was edified.

Now with the understanding of a wife... *The Other* had no husband.

—•••—

It wasn't as if *The One* didn't forgive *The Other*. He did forgive her and he wished her well. It wasn't as if *The One* hadn't acknowledged his own mistakes. He had acknowledged them and regretted them profoundly. But *The One* was determined to never again let a woman exert that much power over him. *The Other* had not truly understood the pain her leaving had caused and the depths of the darkness into which his heart sank. She wasn't privy to his struggles late in the night when the pain was at its apex, and he vowed to make it through and never return.

The weight of her effect on him caught him off guard; *The One* had not realized how deeply rooted *The Other* was in his soul. He discovered that in the wake of her absence, even the simplest things became a chore. Misery and distraction were now his daily companions and *The One* wondered if he'd ever be free. But "never again" he told himself, "never again".

The One remembered that he had told *The Other* that she was perfect and deep down, despite her obvious flaws, he still believed it. But in the matter of his heart he deemed her dangerous, a love that could not be controlled and therefore was to be avoided at all costs. *The One* was determined to move on.

Resolute in his new paradigm *The One* returned himself to the business of work—no play and the safe haven of enterprise—and slowly but surely some of the pain went away.

The One: *I'm going to be okay.*

He reasoned.

The One: *I'm going to be okay.*

Yes, there were times when *The Other's* memory, unsolicited, would dance through his mind, creating a moment of love-sick paralysis, but sooner or later his discipline would kick in and he would remind himself it was over. *The One* had convinced himself that he was safe from her love and the vulnerability that came with it. This worked for weeks, until, one day in his spirit, he heard a still small voice whisper: *She is your wife.*

He argued with himself, offering a vehement debate, and yet…

The Cross bid him surrender.

He was at a business meeting. King of the room, he charmed everyone with his intellect and affability. It was the height of male bonding. Big money and big dreams were there for the taking. The men gathered around the table spoke of enterprise, not love. Nevertheless, in the core of his spirit *The One* heard that same still small voice whisper: *She is your wife.*

He was distracted and it showed. One of the other businessmen asked him, "Are you okay, man?"

The One: Yeah. Yeah, I'm fine. Let's get down to business.

But, still, the Cross bid him surrender.

Often encumbered with the concerns of life, his days were long. Sleep was his only safe haven, and *The One* embraced it like a long-lost friend. But in the middle of his slumber, when the moon cradled the earth before day break, the truth interrupted his rest and again *The One* heard: *She is your wife.*

He dredged up old hurt to fight the revelation but still…

The Cross bid him surrender.

At every social event, Heaven surrounded him with the example of family—couples sharing their lives together with no boundaries and no walls. It was the manifestation of God's promise and, in every example, he saw *The Other,* her hand in his, sharing the defining moments of their lives.

The confirmation flooded him like a tsunami. The words resonated in his spirit even stronger: *She is your wife.*

And in the face of *The One's* remaining doubts...

The Cross, unwavering, bid him surrender.

Then one day, without fanfare or fuss, absent of pomp or flagrant declaration, *he did.*

SIXTH REVELATION

Commentary

*O*ne of the most difficult things in life can be the act of surrender—of letting go, embracing change or allowing God to move us into something unfamiliar. Whether it is a new career, a new relationship, a new direction or new surroundings, change can be scary when our hearts have grown accustomed to the familiar, especially when the shift is sudden and unexpected.

My mother is a walker. She has walked for years as her primary source of exercise. She wakes up at dawn and walks for miles through the illustrious hills of San Gabriel Valley. She uses that time to commune with God and center herself before starting her day. Walking has always been a great joy in her life. However, as she progressed into her senior years, she began to experience serious pain in her knees. As fate would have it, she came to need knee surgery, which drastically impaired her ability to walk as a form of exercise. Characteristic of human nature, she rebelled against this new truth. It was an unwanted change to a routine she loved, so in spite of her doctor's warnings she walked until she aggravated her condition to the point of excruciating pain and was forced to stop. She was miserable. Her beloved walking had been taken away and, with it, the sanctuary of nature that she so enjoyed. Now she spent most of her days at home, sedentary, moping and angry because of the forced change in her life. But as the saying goes, you can't keep a good woman down, and my mom is one of the best.

After she spent an adequate amount of time feeling sorry for herself—equipped with a nagging pep talk from me—she embraced the change in her life and searched for new forms of exercise. She enrolled in a gym and began taking aqua aerobics and a SilverSneakers class (which provides exercises for seniors that they can do from a chair).

She met a host of new friends, lost some weight and never looked back.

Change can be hard, but when we surrender to Christ and trust Him in a new place, we open ourselves up to new blessings. Two years later, my mother's knees were fully healed. She resumed her beloved walking but continued her aqua aerobics classes so she could keep up with all of the new friends she had made. Sometimes, when we surrender, God returns what we thought we lost in a fuller more meaningful way.

When I was engaged to my husband we had quite a few intense discussions about where we would live once we began married life together. We both lived in Los Angeles County but I lived on the west side and he lived on the northern side or "the valley" as we Angelinos call it. As a west-side girl, I always imagined that we would live by the beach after we were married. But Ryan despised the traffic and the congestion of the west side. It was basically a scene from the opening montage of the 1960s television series *Green Acres* and neither one of us was budging.

We debated this for months until finally Ryan put his foot down. Not only were we going to live in the valley, he decided, but we were going to begin married life in his apartment, in an effort to save money. That revelation of course led to a very heated argument. I mean, I was all for us saving money, but I wanted to do it in a new place that we would move into together. I wanted a fresh start! I wanted to break ground in a place that would be new to both of us so that it would intrinsically be "our" space. But he was resolute, and I knew in my spirit that I needed to make peace with his decision, and trust my soon-to-be-husband's leadership and surrender any doubts or misgivings I had to God. And that is exactly what I did. I prayed, I let it go, I took a deep breath and I prepared to move into my husband's place after we were married.

Two weeks before our wedding a new unit opened up in Ryan's apartment building. The building's manager approached my husband and told him that it was on her heart to save it just for us. It was the largest unit in the complex, and they offered to renovate it to our liking. It had a huge kitchen and a fabulous balcony that overlooked the park across the street. We were allowed to move in with no extra fees, at a monthly rate that we could afford. We began our married life in a beautiful apartment that I delighted in every day that we were there.

When I surrendered our housing situation to God and determined in my heart to be happy wherever our new beginning was, God gave me my heart's desire, His way: A gorgeous peaceful place to begin a new life with the love of my life. And not only that, as I got acclimated to my surrounding community I began to prefer the pace and the atmosphere of the valley far more than I did the westside.

The word of GOD in Psalm 9:10 says, *And those who know your name put their trust in you, for you, O Lord, have not forsaken those who seek you.* And in Matthew 16:25, *For whoever would save his life will lose it, but whoever loses his life for my sake will find it.*

God's word assures us that no matter what changes we endure, He will be with us. When we trust and surrender to Christ without inhibition, He can bring a fresh anointing to a situation that once seemed destitute.

My best friend lived in Los Angeles, California, for many years in hot pursuit of an acting career. Though she had some notable career accomplishments, Hollywood never opened its arms to her in the way that her talent warranted. When she got past the acceptable ingénue age, and her mother was becoming increasingly ill from Alzheimer's disease, she made the decision to pick up, move back home to the south and become her mother's primary caregiver. She abandoned her dreams of stardom and decided to trust God for a new beginning.

This change was no easy task. Being a caregiver is an exhausting act of love, and many nights were spent in tears and utter despair. But every day, in spite of her sadness, she kept the faith and continued to trust God for a new beginning. It was not easy and it did not happen overnight but within five years of moving away from Los Angeles, she was married, owned a business with her husband and had started a film production company with two business partners. She also, with the help of her family, was able to find a wonderful home healthcare nurse for her mother, who, as I pen this, is stable and still with us. My best friend sacrificed her fears and her agenda. She chose to believe without seeing and to hope without proof. The result was that everything she strived for in Los Angeles was provided for her in Texas.

As I stated, the act of surrender can be one of life's most difficult challenges. We fight desperately against change or against the realization that we may have reached rock bottom in a particular situation. We either don't want to accept it, or we fear losing control. But God patiently waits for us to relinquish the fight and trust that our rock-bottom can become the solid foundation of His refuge, the place where He gives us our most profound rebound. When you surrender, you have not "given up" the fight; you have "released it" into God's more capable hands. Great is His faithfulness! Surrender all, and let the victory of God engulf you.

SIXTH REVELATION

Journal Questions

Sometimes life's circumstances can usher in a dramatic, sudden change. Other times it is the Spirit of God calling you to make a change.

1) **What change(s) are you having difficulty accepting in your life and why? Or, what change is God directing you to that you are not fully embracing and why?**

_____

_____

_____

_____

_____

_____

_____

_____

_____

_____

_____

_____

_____

_____

_____

_____

_____

2) Write a prayer to God surrendering your fears, doubts and frustrations regarding this change.

3) Now that you have written out a prayer surrendering this change to God, what things can you begin to do differently to fully embrace this change in a positive way?

_____

_____

_____

_____

_____

_____

_____

_____

_____

_____

_____

_____

_____

_____

_____

_____

_____

_____

_____

_____

_____

_____

4) Write about the testimony of someone you know who has endured great change in their life and ended up with a positive outcome.

_____

_____

_____

_____

_____

_____

_____

_____

_____

_____

_____

_____

_____

_____

_____

_____

_____

_____

_____

_____

_____

_____

_____

_____

SIXTH REVELATION

Challenge

Pick something in your sphere of influence that is sorely in need of a definitive change for the better. It can be a project in your home you keep putting off. It can be something needed at your church, at your job, in your community or maybe even at your child's school. Take the initiative and be an agent for change in a positive way. If you're not sure what that thing is, it is the very thing that has been nagging at you and every time that it crosses your path you think, "If this just got fixed, or if somebody would take the time to organize this better, it would make a world of difference". Well...that person is you. Step up to the plate and be the catalyst for a better experience.

SIXTH REVELATION

Growth Check

At this point you should have completed **The Sixth Revelation Questions** as well as your **Sixth Revelation Challenge**. Take some time to reflect on how the changes you have made have specifically affected you and others.

Wow! You have come a mighty long way in just a short amount of time. You have released fears, made bold commitments, forgiven, trusted, walked in love and now embraced change.

I am proud of you. Take pride in your progress as well.

As you embrace change in your life as well as initiate change where you want to see it, take the next few days to journal about your experience. As I stated, change is not always easy. Any progress is a seed sowed. Keep it up! The best is yet to be.

As you take this journey it is important to be cognizant of your growth, and your feelings. If you are taking this journey alone, always take the time to pray and write about your progress. If you are taking this journey within the boundaries of a group of people who are also reading The Dunes, *it is important to pray as a group as well as to share your feelings and progress with each other.*

The spirit of completion beckons us! Let's journey on to The Seventh Revelation and take that final step.

THE SEVENTH REVELATION

GRATITUDE

When you fully understand that the Present Moment is the only one promised and the only one in which you have power, your appreciation soars.

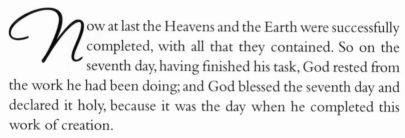

*n*ow at last the Heavens and the Earth were successfully completed, with all that they contained. So on the seventh day, having finished his task, God rested from the work he had been doing; and God blessed the seventh day and declared it holy, because it was the day when he completed this work of creation.

-Genesis 2:1-3

The Other stood in a daze as fuzzy images came slowly into view. She looked around.

The Other: *Where am I?*

The Other looked again. Something about this place felt strangely familiar, but at the same time completely new. And then it dawned on her.

The Other: *The Dunes? I'm at The Dunes?*

It was The Dunes but somehow it was different, transformed. There was no sand, no hill to conquer. No scorching heat. Instead, a gorgeous sunny day engulfed the most beautiful garden she had ever seen. Had it been this way all along?

The Other looked again and found she was encompassed by family and friends. They were smiling and filled with joy. And there, twenty-five feet in front of her, stood *The One*. God's answer to her heart's prayer. He stood waiting to receive her as his own. Now with the understanding of a husband, *The One* offered *The Other* his heart and his life without boundaries and absent of walls. He had surrendered all of his fear and trepidation at the Cross. Now a new man in Christ, *The One* was truly able to care for *The Other* and give all of himself. He knew her gift! Her sunshine could make even his darkest corners bright. With an open heart, *The One* was now free to love *The Other* completely, cherish her as his second self and protect her for life.

Draped in an exquisite white dress, she was breathtaking—the jewel in his crown, his pride and joy. Tears streamed down his face echoing all that was in his heart, and as *The Other* walked toward *The One* they saw only each other, their smiles a testimony to their delight.

Loved ones laughed and rejoiced as the Spirit of the God saturated the atmosphere, making all things good.

With each step she took, *The Other* thought of their love. The destiny that she would now spend in his arms, come what may. How different they were from that first day at The Dunes. God had grown them in spite of themselves, divinely knitting their hearts together and as a carpenter crafting them to be as one. When they met, God knew, when they loved, God knew. And when they doubted, still He knew. This plan, their union, was ineluctably ordained by the sovereignty of His grace—The Master's beauty, their miracle to behold!

Overwhelmed with gratitude, her eyes filled with tears as she realized that in their strength there was nothing they could give that would equal this gift. And so *The Other* said that which was due and so often not spoken.

The Other: *Thank you, Father.*

GOD: It is my good pleasure to bless you.

And with this, God placed her in the arms of her beloved.

Hand in hand, looking into each other's eyes, they vowed to put God first and to love each other unconditionally. Bearing all things, believing all things, hoping all things and enduring all things, the Christ in them would never fail.

The One: *I Do.*

The Other: *I Do.*

God, by his power, made them both, and now by His ordinance He made them one. They promised life and lived it...happily ever after.

THE END
and the beginning.

SEVENTH REVELATION

Commentary

*F*resh out of college and excited about my newly formed adulthood and independence, I moved into a beautiful, gated condo community in Playa Del Rey, the town adjacent to my school. And although I had virtually no credit history and no proof of income, the owner liked me and allowed me to move in no questions asked. The condo-complex was named Cross Creek Village, and it boasted three swimming pools, a full gym, two tennis courts, a playground, a recreation room, a conference room and a dry cleaners located on the property for the residents' convenience. Everyone who came to visit me was always amazed at how beautiful Cross Creek was. Complete with babbling brooks and picture-perfect landscaping, it looked like a small village that had been placed inside of a garden. It was a peaceful majestic oasis, a residential escape whose benefits had, unfortunately, been sorely lost on me.

Don't get me wrong, I loved living at Cross Creek Village, but it wasn't until I moved away that I truly appreciated its grandeur. While I lived there I never used the pools, the tennis courts or the gym. In fact, my only interaction with those amenities was when I had guests and they requested my key so they could gain access to all of Cross Creek's privileges.

I spent my time at Cross Creek running to work or running to try to get more work. My focus was always on tomorrow, and I didn't stop to take stock and realize the favor God had given me, to not only allow me residence in that community but also to live in such a beautiful place. I did not take the time I should have taken to fully appreciate that blessing. Gratitude and appreciation are not only the ways we say thank you, they are the evidence of honor that we bestow on the gift giver as well as the gift.

Nowadays, whether it's stress, immersion in the latest technology or the cares of life, it seems something is always preventing us from being totally "present" in the moment.

How many times have you been somewhere and been more engaged with your phone than with what was actually happening around you? How many times have you put off a social engagement, travel or love because you were waiting to be thinner, richer or whatever else you felt tomorrow might bring? With that paradigm, it's no wonder we find ourselves gratitude-deficient. How can we be grateful for our daily bread when we are constantly focused on tomorrow's loaf?

Tomorrow is not promised. Knowing this to be true, it becomes increasingly foolish to keep our minds fixated on something that isn't even here yet. I am not saying you should stop planning for the future, because that would be foolish as well. What I am proposing is that we not be so focused on what is to come that we don't take the time to appreciate all that is. Simply put, enjoy your Cross Creek while you have it.

———•◆•———

In my early forties, I began going through what is culturally referred to as "the change". It is a time in a woman's life when her hormones rebel against the norm and fluctuate, causing considerable emotional and physical discomfort. It is followed by my all-time favorite, the mind-boggling hormonal weight gain, which is not precipitated by bad eating habits or a lack of exercise. It just appears on your body uninvited. Yeah, it's a fun time all around and to put it bluntly, I was not happy. My stomach, which had once been flat, was now a pudgy soft playground of goo.

My vocabulary, which had once been vast, was now caught up in a perpetual hormonal brain fog, and I despised every moment of it. I hated the weight gain, I loathed the lack of clarity and I detested the private summers. All I wanted was my old body back, immediately.

My husband and I love live music, so we are often out and about supporting local or touring bands. Such was the case the night we found ourselves at The House of Blues in Hollywood, jamming to The Gap Band in concert. I would love to tell you that I was completely present for every glorious moment of that night, but I wasn't. I spent the bulk of the evening inside my head, hating my body, hating perimenopause and lamenting about how things used to be. Every woman who walked in with the waist I used to have fueled the conversation in my mind of all I had lost, as well as musings of what I could possibly do to get it back again. I felt like it would not be until I somehow got things back to the way they used to be that I could enjoy my life and fully live again.

But here's the thing, while I was waiting to "live again"… life was happening. Around me, joy was flowing through the air like oxygen. But instead of partaking in it, I chose to fixate on something that, in that moment, I had no control of. I was standing next to my husband, a man who loves me and my body just the way it is: we were surrounded by good friends and perfect strangers, all cheering, singing and dancing to The Gap Band's old-school hit "Party Train" and I missed it. Life was happening, and I wasn't there! I was in my head preoccupied with self-pity.

I was so focused on a *tomorrow* that is not promised that I let the *now* that was given slip away unappreciated.

What if that moment at The House of Blues had been my last night on earth? I would have spent my last night ungrateful and worried. What a waste of time when I could have spent the night fully engaged and present in the blessings that surrounded me. A husband who loves me unconditionally, friends who were happy to see me, jamming to a funky phenomenal band.

How much time do we lose waiting to live? How much do we never truly experience because we are not fully present in the gift that is each new day?

In The Seventh Revelation, we see our couple basking in the glow of *the promise*, grateful for the divine providence of God and enjoying the blessing of the moment surrounding them. They see that, all along, even through their turmoil and struggle, God's plan was at work.

We are a blessed people, rich because we serve a God who is merciful and faithful. Don't waste time waiting for life to begin—it has! Appreciate the day and be grateful for all that God has already done.

SEVENTH REVELATION

Journal Questions

1) List twenty-five things you are grateful for and why. Include anything you can think of, from the smallest blessings to the most profound.

_____

_____

_____

_____

_____

_____

_____

_____

_____

_____

_____

_____

_____

_____

_____

_____

_____

_____

_____

_____

2) Which one of the things on your list have you been the least appreciative of and in a sense have taken for granted? And with this realization what are you now prepared to do about it?

_____

_____

_____

_____

_____

_____

_____

_____

_____

_____

_____

_____

_____

_____

_____

_____

_____

_____

_____

_____

_____

_____

_____

_____

_____

_____

_____

3) Pretend that today is your last day on earth. Who would you want to spend it with and what would you want to do? (You will find that the answer to this question may bring a clarity that might surprise you.)

4) Still pretending that today is your last day on earth, what relationship do you wish you would have cultivated more and what accomplishment do you wish you would have taken the time to achieve?

5) Let's bring our focus back to the blessing of the day. What relationship in your life are you most proud of and why? What accomplishment in your life are you most proud of and why?

_____

_____

_____

_____

_____

_____

_____

_____

_____

_____

_____

_____

_____

_____

_____

_____

_____

_____

_____

_____

_____

_____

_____

_____

_____

_____

Thank you for taking the time to answer those very sobering questions. No one likes to think of their last day on earth but I wanted you to come face to face with what is really important to you and what legacy you would like to leave. The good news is: You still have time to build those relationships and accomplish those goals.

SEVENTH REVELATION

Challenge

This week we are going to pay homage to the 70s and the 80s. When you are in the presence of another human being, do not look at your phone to check messages, texts or emails. Do not play on your iPad, Kindle or any other type of tablet or e-readers. Do not access any type of social media in the presence of another person. You will give that moment and that individual your undivided attention. You will be fully present even if you are in the check-out line at the grocery store. The only exception is a work-related need. However, outside of work, as long as another human being is in your vicinity, you are not to access or use any technology (phone, tablet or social media). Remember, this day, this moment, is your gift. I challenge you to experience it in full.

After this challenge and beyond, I urge you to apply everything you have learned and continue to make positive changes for the better. Put God first, embrace life fully, be grateful for the day, stand up for what you believe in, love unconditionally, be a blessing in a life other than your own and forgive because someday soon you will need it in return. Most importantly, divorce fear...marry faith and make it the best relationship of your life!

SEVENTH REVELATION

Growth Check

At this point you should have completed **The Seventh Revelation Questions** as well as started on the journey to fully applying your **Seventh Revelation Challenge**. Take some time to write in your journal about your experience. Or take a moment to quietly reflect on the following questions:

What has this journey revealed to you about yourself that you didn't already know?

In what ways has this journey grown your walk with Christ and impacted your outlook on life?

As you faithfully examine all you have to be grateful for, journal about your experience and the steps you are taking to make a conscious effort to appreciate the blessings of the day.

As you take this journey it is important to be cognizant of your growth, and your feelings. If you are taking this journey alone, always take the time to pray and write about your progress. If you are taking this journey within the boundaries of a group of people who are also reading The Dunes, *it is important to pray as a group as well as to share your feelings and progress with each other.*

Congratulations on completing *The Dunes!*

It is my sincere prayer that you find you are a different person than you were when you began this journey. Try The Dunes again in 6 to 12 months. Next time dig a little deeper and grow even more full bodied in the things of God.

A LETTER FROM ERIN

*Hope deferred maketh the heart sick: but when the
desire cometh, it is a tree of life.* -Proverbs 13:12

During our journey together, I have encouraged you to let go of
fear, to love and to commit unconditionally, to trust, to forgive
and to expect blessings. In many ways, in my own life, these have
been my challenges. I have had to learn to trust God for hope
deferred, love without walls and expect great things in the face
of less-than-stellar odds. It is not easy. But it is a choice we must
make every day.

Growing up I was raised by a wonderful mother who
sacrificed a great deal so that I would not know lack. However,
although my father and I mended our relationship in my adult
years and became good friends, growing up, my father abandoned
me physically, emotionally and financially. As a result, there were
always dual messages floating around in my head, one of love and
one of abandonment. So when it came time for me to enter a
relationship, although I loved with my whole heart and gave of
myself completely, when problems arose, I would leave because I
was terrified of being left.

I had to learn to "be" what I desired in a relationship. If I
wanted someone who was going to persevere through adversity
I had to become someone who persevered through adversity.
I needed to sow what I wanted to reap. Likewise the word of
God is activated through faith and action. My fear and doubt

regarding my life only served to harvest more things to be fearful and doubtful of. When I changed my mind, God changed my life.

As I shared in The First Revelation, I reached my late thirties, looked around and found my life was in ruins, and from that moment forward, I literally made a decision to simply and completely believe God. When His word says goodness and mercy shall follow me all of the days of my life, I believe Him. When His word says He will never leave me or forsake me, I believe Him. The day I chose to take His word personally was the day my life began to expand in a blessed and miraculous way.

I chose the Proverbs verse above because it is true in all facets; hope deferred does make the heart sick. But I also chose it because it says "when the desire cometh" it is a tree of life. This means that the desire of our heart, lined up with His will, is coming and when it comes it will be a tree of life. The tree of life is revealed in the book of Genesis, chapter 2:9. It is the tree God placed in the center of the Garden of Eden. As the God-placed desire in your heart manifests, it will be a tree of life for you, a central place from which you bear much fruit. For the Lord, our God, is the vine and we are the branches. If we remain in Him and He in us, we will bear much fruit, but apart from Him we can do nothing.

God's plan for your life is marvelous and if you surrender to Him, He will grow you in spite of yourself. You will look up one day and notice that your "Dune" has become a splendid garden. Know your steps are ordered and that there is a divine providential plan for your life. It has been unfolding since the moment you took your first breath.

God sees you.

He has plans for you.

...And

neither His word nor His plans return to Him void.
Believe it.

God bless!
Much Love,

Erin Sands

ACKNOWLEDGEMENTS

I am so grateful to God for giving me the diary of *The Dunes*. It is my love letter to Christ, my testimony, my journey thus far. I am grateful for the guidance and creative inspiration of the Holy Spirit. I will forever stand on the rock of Christ, boldly declaring to all who will listen that He is the way, the truth and the light.

Thank you to all of my friends and family who encouraged me to write and repeatedly affirmed my gifts. Your faith has been a life raft; a steadfast extension of God's love and I appreciate it more than words can say. Thank you, Sherea, Celeste, Nicole, Jason and Charles...the courageous and wonderful "first responders" of *The Dunes*, who opened their lives and allowed *The Dunes* in their hearts. Your public testimonies are a blessing to everyone. Thank you to my mother, Brenda Anderson, to whom this book is dedicated. Where would I be without your love? You are my angel. Thank you for always believing in me. Thank you to my wonderful editors, Lauren Ruiz and Jessica Bryan. You ladies make me look good!

Thank you to my beloved husband, my best friend, my heart... Ryan Sands. Our laughter is the best part of every day. Thank you for clothing me daily in your unconditional love. When I felt ugly and wanted to hide you gave me your hand and made your heart my safe haven. When I felt sassy and ready to soar, you cheered me on and encouraged me every step of the way. Our marriage is God's way of showing off His faithfulness and I am forever grateful.

Made in the USA
San Bernardino, CA
01 June 2014